A Rainbow by Night

Vudu Amor

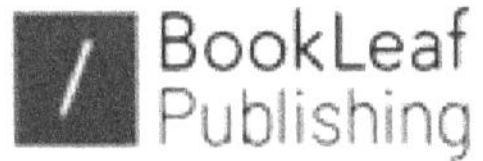

Presentation by *BookLeaf Publishing*

Web: www.bookleafpub.com

E-mail: info@bookleafpub.com

ISBN : 9789357211291

First edition 2022

DEDICATION

Dedicated to unconditional love, understanding and faith.

ACKNOWLEDGEMENT

Family, friends and all that assisted in the creative process. Most of all I would truly like to thank you, the reader.

PREFACE

Twenty years ago I was published for the first time. Out of all the drugs I have tried, the feeling of holding my written wordThe Truth Is, in print form was certainly the greatest high of all time. I had given breath to something that was all my own, full of potential as it would travel from hand to hand, eye to eye, mouth to mouth, mind to mind. The thought of my creation being in the world along with the hopes that I had for it was pure euphoria. Now, I have had the chance to once again give rise to something in which the same high and pregnant expectations exist, only this time I am even more elated.

You see, 20 years ago, what I felt was my greatest work at the time Buried Alive was not allowed to be a part of the continuing collection. Iwasdeemedtohavemisleading, non-substantiated accusations. In my naivety of youth I didn't push back or argue, something was better than nothing, so I went along and omitted Buried Alive.A few weeks later, I discovered that the information has been substantiated through declassified documents. I discovered the truth of everything comes in due time. Every entrance is measured precisely.

I embarked on this challenge to come full circle. To include Buried alive without censorship, in addition to adding on to the countless other truths that I have encountered over the last twenty years.

There is a saying do the smallest of things with the greatest passion. Here I have put as much love into the small words as I have the complex. The same devotion resides in both the shallow thoughts and profound ideas. Sometime the words don't flow out of me just right, know that each and every letter was crafted with love and devotion. It is my hope that the reader will enjoy A Rainbow by Night and recognize the love and devotion that I speak of.

-Vudu

Mi Amor

Sitting here
on the banks
of the king james river
I don't know what poetry is
All these years
She still puzzles me

Reminding me of her
dualistic mysteries
After the spoken words
Days, hours, minutes, months
In classrooms
writing anywhere that would listen

Hey man!
You sound like Gill Scott Herron
before I had awareness
of who the artist was

I thought I knew
knew what poetry was
the heartbeat of the inner verse
spirit of stars everlasting
kissed by heaven's bliss
inhabitants of the Poseidons Abyss

walking on dry land

I am grateful
to be learning her
contours and curves
Her steady, seductive stride
As the pen glides across the page
Orgasmically studying every word
upon my truest lovers lips

Ancient Future of her features
her mentalism
classical correspondence
tone and vibration
method and meter
Pulsating polarities
Her mood melody
gender and agenda
rhythms that rhyme
the cause she effects

Thrice Great

I thought I knew
new what poetry was
But I am Loki(ed) every time
...by...
her inward communication

Beginning to End

A blind person sees his true self
The seeing put forth-false images
Mirrored by a new sun
seen in the eyes of the father
time is still born
The beginning is the end

Where does the end begin?
How do you view yourself?
Looking like your father
created in his image
Men and women are born
and start to walk away from the sun

Commence to worship the sun
A means to an end
Sharing the faith of your father
What matter is the image?
The age of a new Era is born
Mother Earth will we ever look inside
ourselves?

Who change the image
from mother to son?
She was there when u were born

Only faith's eyes can see your father
I'm not sure myself
My mind lies within
Alpha and Omega

Mystical Illusion

Our vision is being sold to us
72 inches
reality plastered faces
microchipped minds
flat round up-side down
rich poor-peace and war
right wrong white and black

trash is in the treasure

pleasure in pain
the insane sane
brain; heart or gut feeling
he-motions swimming in plastic oceans
black circus mirrors

true healers verses Rockefeller laws
lonely applause in amphitheaters of hallowed
bones
stones and sticks
glass bricks
printed on golden paper
caitiff saviors

later now

take a bow
before the show starts
entertainment's Arc

brand new artifacts

Unholy Reality

Master not Slave

We fall prey to our sense of limitations
when we value ourselves
based on outside sources
Neither the stars, past lives, nor karma
can rule us in the least
when we realize
we are children of the Creator

At any moment
it is our mind
that determines
what will happen to us
gain power over your mind
refuse to let it rule you
the hammer doesn't swing the hand
the slave toils for the master
and the soil provides for both

Claim with authority
You divine birthright
Food medicine gurus and shamans
have no power
besides that which you
invest in them
you create them to tell your mind

what the essence of your being
already knows

You can shine brighter than the stars
your mana is love
your medicine forgiveness
your healer your inner self
The only belief you need is
you deserve love

This world can give you nothing
you do not already have
the smallest thoughts add up
like grains of sand form a beach
lessons we don't understand
and grow old to obtain
memories that remain
a whisper in the wind
others that hold us tighter
then our closest friend

Shadows illuminated by the suns movement
the Earth is moving
even as we are standing still
she is taking us somewhere
and just like a child
we don't care
we will be happy
just to get there

I Do...

I do as I was taught
I do as I have learned
I do as I have seen
I do as I have heard
I do by doing whatever it is I am doing
      Even if it's screwing
      Even if it's cheating
      Even if it's smoking
I do what you tell
I do what you ask
I do what you expect
I do what you accept
I do as you do--whatever it is you do
      Even if its lying
      Even if it's stealing
      Even if it's killing
I need to do what I feel
But do what feels good
I need to do good
But good don't feel good
Pleasure is in sin
That's why the devil wins

Today 4/22/2022

power-up
power-up

rise

power-up
power-up

rise

power-up
power-up

rise

lift those phenomenal eyes
to baby blue skies

50 Shades of Blue
(Vishuddha)

Linguistics perspective perceptions
enhancing cognitive awareness

more blues you know
more blues you see

Imperial midnight jagged ice
star command lapis lazuli

Regal turquoise shadow light
Sapphire steel baby Honolulu

Egypt was one of the first
Representing Blessed Virgin's birth

Throughout man's Renaissance
boys adorned the cast

Where sky and ocean greet
endless possibilities meet

If there were no words for time
How could it bind

Indigo blood clairaudience
Royal pigmented power suits

Extrasensory visualizations
what does Allah dream

Beyond Oblivion
Synchronistic Paradigm shifts

Spinning wheels of tranquility
Astral auras of wisdom and peace

Turkish robin's egg morning
Carolina Cobalt Oxford Yale

Electric Jazz pigeon aquamarine
curious cornflower Tiffany teal

Depth trust stabilities confidence
Sincerity spawning intuition's imagination

Denim arctic admiral chrysocolla
Hydrangeas forget-me-not peacock

Persian chalcedony sodalite New York
Dodger navy seagull Kansas City

No matter the hue
our spectrums are all blue

The Lotus that Grew from Concrete

The match that sparked the flame
Panther Power
Apocalypse Now
Strictly for my
Never
Ignorant
Getting
Goals
Accomplished

Only the ancestors can judge this lotus
that grew from a crack in the concrete
flying without wings
learning the melodies
caged nightingales sing

Great 400 year old incarcerated rage
what would you do for love
blasphemy military minds
us against the world

Only Allah can judge this lotus that grew
from a crack in the concrete

without a native tongue
learning how to teach
uplifting, empowering the weak

Still we rise
changes after so many tears
all eyez on the prize
better ways create better dayz

Only She can judge this lotus that grew
from The Great Dismal Swamp
without roots
learning to build
cities of refuge
channeling souls from Moses Grandy Trail

I wonder if heaven got a project
eugenics experiment
this is a letter to our unborn
Brenda aborted her baby

Only God can judge the lotus that grew

Her greatest fear of life
Raising a son
without a husband
not even a boyfriend

I ain't mad at cha

hail Afeni for not doing the same
thank Mother Africa for Dr. Mutulu Shakur's
cures
baby don't cry we got the secrets to war

Only Jah can judge this lotus that grew from a
crack in the concrete
without feet running; the streetz
Giving that God body speech

Letter to the pope
hit em up
dear mama raised a hell raiser
smile Black Jesus

And that's the fin I suppose
unless you question
R U still down for me

All my love is for u

Why must I love you
you love someone else
Is it possible
that I love you
While you are
Hugging another
Kissing another
Holding another
someone
anyone
Tell me how

Your head
on their chest
Love love love
My mind can not find rest
Who do you caress
Comfort from the daily stress
Why must I love you
when you love another

How can I love you so
when you think I am invisible
Cast away in the middle of the day

Why do I love you
How can I love you
Can I truly love you
when your heart is with another
Should I care for you
as you are sharing covers with another
Lovers that never touch
Only their eyes meet
But in their hearts they....

The Oceans Last Wave

Every single word possesses its own
legends
coming together like you and me

Me We

together we are that floetry
super stars of planetary alignment
lighthouses for all to sea

Me We

Muhammad Ali
rumble in the concrete jungle
standing against tyranny

Me We

Patience over power
endurance wears out strength
see with your ears
hear with your eyes

Me We

Our opponents are strong
But there is nothing to fear

Me We UNITY

Little Prince

truth tricks the senses
hearts see what the eyes can not
why live in a box
when the multiverse is open

dreams
Invisible essentials
cherish them
they may show you

how to heal
thy self
and the planet earth

Buried Alive

Cocking the hammer back, easing the barrel into my mouth, lips and teeth clinging to the cold-hearted steel, as if my lungs depended on the gun for air, slowly closing my eyes, audaciously waiting, with my finger wrapped loosely around the trigger. Briefly empowered! J. Freeman controlled his own destiny; no other faction would have the opportunity to abort his ambitions, assassinate his civil liberties; or crucify his God given convictions-his existence residing solely in his hands, his hands alone. Cold sweat rolled down my face dripping on my shivering gun wielding arm. Surrounded by darkness. I sat with my life in my hands.

After the surge of strength subsided, a weakness methodically crept through my body, like sap oozing from a maple tree. What would drive a person to commit the ultimate act-drugs, war, poverty? Maybe the inhuman actions I see transpiring before me are just the way of the world; however, it is this path society travels that make me abandon all hope for my, and the world's future. So, the only solution I can concoct is this fatal head shot. One shot would end my torment, one shot would put me to rest,

one shot would slay the sleepiness that slumber
could not cure.

Trapped! A Blackmale-blackmailed;
blackballed, on a blacklist. Society hates me
and I am well aware of this, I know this, because
society is trying to teach me to hate myself.
Society has bleached me, whitewashed me, only
to inevitably to die black. Modern civilization
hates the color of my skin, the blood in my
veins, the true knowledge locked deep inside my
brain-wisdom of millenniums without chains,
stolen legacies translated in Plato's name
(Egyptian knowledge transformed into Greek
philosophy). Biblical names changed and
rearranged. Society hates me because it fears
me in my essential form, my righteousness is
contagious-look though the eyes of a Panther
and see J Edgar Hoover sucking the life out of
Malcolm X and with the same bullet murdering
Dr. Martin Luther King and crippling the civil
rights movement, conveys that America does
want the tired, the poor, or those yearning to
breath free.

Constitutionally she constitutes that a
Blackman is not a whole man, but three-fifths of
a man, calling him a savage Godless beast, and
on the same corner preaches all men are created
equally by the size of his wallet. Civil wars
fought for four years, America's negro, has been

fighting that same war-for more then 400 years.
I know this system despises me because of the
Vietnam veterans who served as human shields,
only to return home, not war heroes, still second
class citizens, consoled with misleading purple
hearts.

In this pop-a-pill I shall be better
tomorrow,society we often settle for temporary
relief (recreational sex, hypnotic drugs, quick
money, fast food) instead of permanent
satisfaction(true love, mental meditation, proper
understanding, healthy eating). Concealed in the
Matrix-pulling the trigger would be like taking
the blue pill, escaping this sane-madness, killing
my numbed pain, dulling this unreal reality; or I
can take the red pill put the gun down and live
life for what it truly is-a black hole that
consumes all.

Damn! It's so easy, one jerk of a trigger, one
less nigger, the spread of AIDS twenty million
and counting. My hand is on the gun fearing the
wars to come, because in places like South
Africa, China, and Russia people are still
fighting for their freedom. Terrorized by
viruses, hints of biological warfare. Me putting
a bullet through my skull wouldn't help the
starving little girl or boy, living in America, in
an age where we are able to travel to the moon
and send satellites across the universe. I could

die here, on my hands and knees, or I could stand tall and fight the battle begun in Genesis.

My finger becomes tense, I become angry; in my millisecond of salvation others would find eternal damnation, my freedom would mean nothing for the millions who remain, wage slaves living day to day, isolated, chained in mental bondage. My problem solving is problem causing to all who cared about me the most; even in death I would find no peace, while my pain ended, others suffering would never cease. No! I refuse to fall prey to this hypocritical nation that sells prescription medication(with millions of side effects at ridiculous prices) with unsure insurance applying to those needing it least. Refusing to be the victim of a Nation where 25% of the population produces 75% of people incarcerated- so-called Rehabilitation, is nothing more then disablement, leaving ex-convicts unable to vote, unable to get a well paying job, unable to remove the steel bars that remain, long after release from the man-zoo.

Sparking my lighter, opening my eyes, lighting my port, I inhale then exhale poison, slowly burying myself in a coffin of ashes, knowing that things must get worse before they get better. Believing that one man and his faith can change the world.

Oracles

David and Goliath
stumbling blocks
throwing stones
obstacles inspire miracles
circumstances move mountains
mustard seeds grow orchards
the eye of the storm
always remains calmest

Rise with the sun
no matter what
how many times
Rise
Rise
shine thy inner light

Bright
Bright
Supernova
Steal away thy night

Shine
Shine
Sight to the blind
Of the 3rd eye kind

healing with rhythm
that's moves the ocean

Sankofa
Sankofa
always move forward

Roots in darkness
makes flowers
Food and Prana
Beautiful tapestries
Under Crystal lakes

Topaz sapphires
Emeralds rubies
diamonds and pearls
gold copper
silver and nickel

Mine thy darkness
Will equals faith
Gods of a crucified shore
Awake!

Spiders silk is stronger then steel

I have seen the wind
ran with it
as it went
Rushing through my locks

Honeysuckle and mulberries
Glide delicately on airs
ballroom floor
Someone has planted rosemary nearby
prancing with a fresh
summer's rain

They hurry to catch
the Azalea blooms and sassafras
Whirling swiftly amongst the leaves

Watching the breeze
open interdimensional doors
twilight on sea Shores

I have seen the win

6221 Osage Avenue

Rough winds
carry gentle summers chills
Sometimes to bright we shine
golden complexions dimmed
by nature; chance; or magic
eternal belongings
earthly ambrosia
death's immortal breath

Long live
Long live
the collective soul
Fairy-mans toll
though Hades Odyssey
Epics of a Supernova

Big Bang
She rose
paths for us to follow

Presence of noon
Blood, sweat, and goodbyes
Amazing grace
Whitey on the moon
The lost are found

in the back of the bus
Resurrecting the fall of Man
Genes of Isis strand

Priceless experiences
Trail of Tears under a starry night
in the midst of a Red Summer
Rage extinguishing hell's fire
birth of a new earth
the last already first
Spreading salvation seeds

Flesh composed of stardust
american nightmares
on old dusty roads
Paved with gold
innerstanding the truth about us
Jesus
Justification of evil
How would Shakespeare be different
If he wrote about atomic bombs?

Moors and Nukes

Fresh water from glistening streams
bear the taste of strange fruits
forbidden leaves falling
as they dig up the roots
which will blow first
Moors or nukes

loathing carnage fed to troops
bare footed soldiers
Mercenaries without boots
borders of slaughter and fences
great wall of Palestine
holy mount Zion crying
to rolling Roman hills

Close the window
there's nothing to see here
inside Chernobyl's glittering ashes
dust to flesh
the rage of a trillion suns
thrown overboard to lighten diaspora's load

snow capped Himalayas
melting; flowing; flooding

Fukushima valley's
with corporate corruption
black dollar signs
gray collar war crimes

Mockingjay no longer sing
They scream
we to have voices
Oh man!!!
with such beautiful minds
what stopped you from hearing mines

scarred shadows of eons Three Mile Islands
the hills have eyes
in the waste lands
New Mexico's desserts
trinity watching
the undiscovered self
taking a quantum leap
backwards

all the earth
once was your shrine
but your new age marvels
have left you blind
so bask in the glory
of your fire this time

Black Abyss

Judas

          Abernathy
          Lancelot
          Benedict
          George Tyler
          ONeal

get your hands off our profits
keep your slimy lips
off their golden cheeks
praising with palms
on a sunday
lynched with sliver the following
week

His-story is Now

sambos
30 coins tell prophets
not to grow
convincing the seers
that they dont know

Now is the Story

repeating itself
digital daydreaming
Hopi hymns
rain dancing
chanting
which actor are you?

Nova

Quiet as kept
the great king slept
Camelot wept
in the distance
land of Avalon

greener pastures in the valley
still waters run deep
Jehovah is God
thy staff and thy rod
taking flight on a
gloomy, cold, rainy
Saviors Day night

I have cried everyday
since that day
although there are no tears to wipe away

You gave us a light to inspire to become
true love to explore
teaching different definitions
of the arts
combative skills from the heart

the strength of your smile

security and kindness
covered in laughter
a joyful atmosphere
when you were near

Elevated friendships to kinship
I wish there were more like you
and this would not make you
any less valuable

Thank you for being
a great son, father , brother
Sensei student and friend

Our hearts are
forever more one
Until we meet again
it has been
an honor and a blessings
to call u brother and friend

this is not the end
it is where our stories begin again

Rise in power
Sleep in peace
You will always be loved
One of lifes masterpieces

Donnell Hopskin

False profits

In this cage I feel powerless
insignificantly weak
hours are days
days turn to weeks
months become unbearable years

time seems subjective
submerged in subconscious
anxiety, depression, and fear
the only weather here

no sun
no moon
Valhalla's stars do not shine
only mankind's
no thunder clapping
no dancing naked in the rain

I close my eyes
the shower transmutes
feeling the mist
from Niagara Falls
squawks and squalls
of seagulls

just me
33 other men
steel bars
encased in
concrete aggression
diamond pressured, brittle rage

directed at any and everything
especially if it has
the same reflection as you
smiling playing jester
for you know who
reciting
Psalms 22

Lethal Injection

The devil lives in my community
some call him crack
living off the sweat of the working man's back
holding hostage those with weak minds
toxic addiction woven into the fabric of time
menace to society afflicting all people

Handicapping the will of God's people
worshiped in the community
late night is her prime time
Whore of Babylon named molly
latest chain enslaving youth's minds
fresh whip blistering backs

Once taken few turn back
zombies formerly people
controlled minds
destroying communities
small white assassins percs
handcuffed time

Ture dealers never do time
they press down the poor man's back
pushing a hope that cracks
the strength of a chosen people

weakening the unity of every community
mass polluters of minds

mangled minds
abandoning time
making sure there is crime in the community
We have to turn our backs
forsaken people
plagued by ex
Falling through the cracks
warped minds
resting at defeat of the people
running time
breaking backs
soon there will be no community

We must come together as one people
to fight the monstrosity-the war on drugs
we must shake this monkey off our backs
when is the time to act-now is the time, while we
still have time

Wow

Eye opening transcended fruit
from crown to root
alluring apocalypse cash
neurotic naked passionate needs
in multiple poses and positions

poet sutra
intramural yoga
Rainbow tantra
Breathing consciously
to become more flexible
Rising in love with something new daily

Climactic Joys and bloody tears
Unification of consciousness
Spontaneous celestial experiences
Enhancing our ESP as we generate DMT
Manifesting universes and galaxies
a sacred Oasis for heaven

Energetically Scripting Love Faces
Hieroglyphics written on Subterranean chamber
walls
Throne of creation
Foreplay chakra stimulation

Yoni eggs and strawberries

Pre-programming Prana
Before we jamming in the name of the lord
Natural Mystic music
Primordial Kaleidoscopes
of hopes, dreams and wishes
Rhythm In the Heat of the Night
Intertwined by candle illumination

Exploring alluring passionate levels
Aphrodite's zenith
Superior uniqueness
Yin yang zig zag zig
Science and Magic
Figurative and abstract
Masculine turn feminine
Vice versa

Us

No self
No me
No you

Us

Pass the lust
so our souls could discuss

what our native tongues
failed to communicate
Our ears would not comprehend
Divine holy Sensations
Seductions satisfaction
Touched intimately
ecstasy's erogenous zone

flow

flow

flow